CW00687611

STEAMING THROUGH CORNWALL

Peter Hay

MP Middleton Press

First published June 1994

ISBN 1 873793 30 8

© Middleton Press 1994

Cover design Deborah Goodridge

Published by Middleton Press
            Easebourne Lane
            Midhurst
            West Sussex
            GU29 9AZ
            Tel: (0730) 813169
(From 16 April 1995 - (01730) 813169)

Printed & bound by Biddles Ltd,
            Guildford and Kings Lynn

CONTENTS

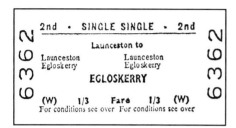

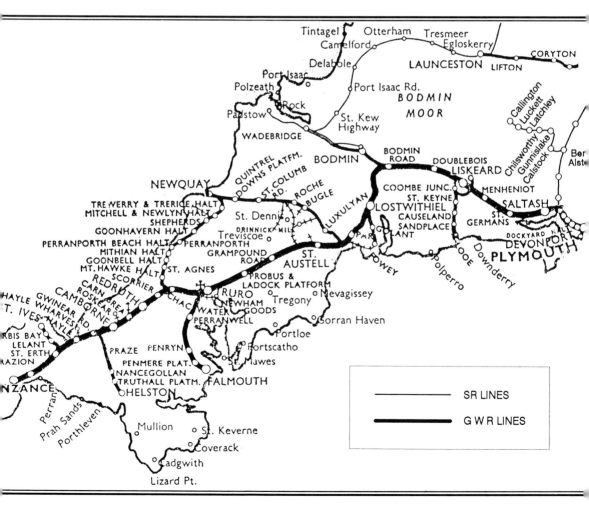

INDEX

INTRODUCTION

Most of the pictures in this book were taken for the same reason as those in my other Middleton Press albums: to record the railway scene before it changed forever. In Kent the threat was electrification; in Sussex and Hants., closure. Down in Cornwall it was the coming of diesel traction which was going to change things. My efforts to record steam in the west before it was too late eventually produced another dividend: pictures at places which lost their railway entirely in the closures of the 1960s. Having visited the local "Mecca" (Wadebridge) in 1957 to photograph celebrities in the shape of the near-legendary "Beattie Well Tanks" as well as the LSWR T9s and O2s, most of my 1959 trip was devoted to getting a picture of a steam train at every GWR station and halt in Cornwall. Apart from locations where there was by then no passenger station, like Truro (Newham) and the china clay branches, I missed only Truthall Platform and Probus & Ladock. A more significant omission from my pilgrimage - sacrificed because my holiday was running out of time and South Devon beckoned - was a photogaphic visit to the SR "Withered Arm", the North Cornwall line from Launceston to Padstow. So I have had to draw upon the collections of others who did not miss their opportunity, for views of those lonely outposts of Waterloo's empire. Their names are credited to the individual pictures and I record here my sincere thanks to them for allowing their work to be shown.

Despite the efforts of the Southern Railway, the GWR was the major railway in Cornwall, and the first part of the book covers its main line from the Tamar to Penzance. Over the years the Great Western built and acquired several branches south of the main line, and they come next, followed by routes north of the main line, two of which had their origins in the Cornwall Minerals Railway. Lastly, but by no means least, we look at the SR (formerly LSWR) in Cornwall.

Maybe it is an indication of how well the GWR invested in the Cornish part of its system that in 1959, when most of these pictures were taken, you had to look quite hard to find any BR standard equipment, even though it was a full decade after nationalisation. Of locomotives, only the heaviest like "Kings" and eight-coupled tender engines normally did not cross the Tamar. The only BR standard engines seen were the newly arrived diesels. The "Cornish Riviera" was BR stock, but few other trains had any. Signalling was, as I recall, exclusivley GWR lower quadrant semaphore. A very close look indeed at any of the station pictures will be required to find any equipment that didn't originate with the old company. The whole scene had a timeless appearance.

The history of Cornwall's railways, of the engines, carriages and wagons that ran on them, of the signals and the stations, had been exceedingly well documented. As well as large scale works like MacDermott's History of the GWR, Dendy Marshall's similar work on the SR, and William's History of the LSWR, there are scores of other books, some of which examine small parts of the Cornish railway system in great detail. So there are plenty of reference sources if you want to know more about the scenes which follow.

There is a bias in my selection of these pictures: where I had to decide between a main line picture and one at some quieter spot, I have chosen the latter. Also, I have deliberately left out pictures of trains in Cornwall's glorious countryside in favour of views at stations, because this book in its small way tries to be some record of what has gone. Which brings me to the captions. I have tried to point out things which seem to me unusual, and things once commonplace which are now seen no longer. To the knowledgeable who already recognize and know what I describe, my apologies. Where I have ignored things or could have described them better, I ask your indulgence, and patience where I have go it wrong. Accuracy has been my aim, but time is dimming the memory.

Finally as always I wish to thank those who have contributed pictures to fill my gaps, and to Neil Stanyon who read the proofs.

Peter Hay
Hove 1994

THE GWR MAIN LINE

Although we think of Cornwall as once famous for its tin mines, it was in fact copper mining which brought its first railways. Because one ton of copper needed eighteen tons of coal for smelting, it was cheaper to move the copper ore to the coal, and Swansea in South Wales became a great copper smelting centre. Deep mining also needed coal for steam pumping engines and in the early years of the last century the roads in the Cornish mining districts were quite incapable of carrying the tonnage between mines and ports. The Hayle Railway of 1837 was the oldest constituent of the GWR main line in Cornwall, as old as the GWR itself. It ran from Hayle to Redruth, and to Portreath on the north coast, traversing a major mining district. By 1843 they were running passenger trains, such was the desire for better communications. This led to the formation of the West Cornwall Railway, opened in1852 from Truro to Penzance, taking over the Hayle Railway. In the process they built a new line avoiding the two previous gravity inclines at Penponds and Angarrack. The WCR was "narrow" (standard) gauge, but when the broad gauge Cornwall Railway reached Truro from the east in 1859, the older company had no money to lay a third rail for broad gauge trains. It was therefore taken over by the GW, South Devon, and Bristol & Exeter Railways which had a natural interest in a complete line of communication to the west. (The Cornwall Railway's finances were as shaky as those of the WCR.) Through traffic was broad gauge but much local traffic between Truro and Penzance remained faithful to the narrow gauge, which triumphed in 1892 when the broad gauge was abolished.

Although continuing rails westwards from Plymouth was an obvious strategy, there was a major difficulty. Even in an industrial district - which Cornwall then was - money was short. In 1850 Brunel wrote from London to a Cornish acquaintance "I have daily been expecting to hear something from you about the Cornwall. Is anything doing, or are we taking another nap?" Besides raising the money, bridging the Tamar was the other great problem. The Royal Albert Bridge took six years to build, but when it was done the chain of rail communication was complete, from Paddington to Penzance. The Cornwall Railway ran from Plymouth to Truro and on to Falmouth, with the WCR continuing from Penwithers Junction, west of Truro, through Hayle to Penzance. By 1889 all this belonged to the GWR, for even though they were only built as single lines with wooden viaducts, the Cornish companies had never prospered enough to carry the cost of their construction. The copper and tin mines were failing fast and mass tourist traffic was still a long way in the future. It took the GWR nearly 40 years to rebuild all the viaducts and double the track from Saltash to Penzance. The Grouping in 1923 did not affect the GWR in Cornwall, and it all passed to BR in 1948. Towards the end of the 1950s the diesels were coming to displace steam, but despite several alarms in the 1960s the main line remains open to Penzance, although many of the wayside stations have closed, as detailed in the captions.

BRITISH TRANSPORT
COMMISSION (W)

SECOND CLASS
Holiday Runabout Ticket
CHILD (1 Week)
No. 114 ——— Rate 9/3

M...ɑʋₑᵥ PRIESTLEY

From............51...to

Available between the Stations shown
on the other side by the routes indicated

Issued subject to the Regulations and
Conditions in the Commission's Publica-
tions and Notices applicable to British
Railways, is
NOT TRANSFERABLE
and must be given-up-on or before the
date of expiry.

TRURO

1. There was once an intensive Plymouth suburban service along the main line, with the down platform at Saltash as its western terminus. The steam rail-motors which started in 1904 created so much business that Autotrains, with a tank engine working pull and push, had taken over by 1914. 0-6-0 pannier tank no. 6419 with four coaches is waiting at Saltash, ready to start back for Plymouth in 1959. The nearest coach is no. W229W, built by BR in 1951 to a GW design.

2. Cornwall daily sent large quantities of milk to London and other places, at first in churns and latterly in rail tanks. No. 6875 *Hindford Grange* is making for Plymouth and points east with milk tanks on the afternoon on 18th August 1959. The up side station buildings here at St. Germans owe much to Brunel's design, with deep eaves and the end bay window. The station nameboard on the lamppost is in blue enamel with white letters, very much a survival by this date.

3. Stone from the nearby granite quarry fills the first three wagons of this local freight working as it leaves Menheniot and crosses the viaduct on its way to Plymouth. A member of the GWR 5700 Class 0-6-0PT is in charge. In the background we can see the down platform building, a pure Brunel design with its roof projecting as an awning all round the structure.

4. No. 7816 *Frilsham Manor* heads a down local goods working over the viaduct at the east end of Liskeard station.   Old bull head rails are laid on their sides and used as check rails beside the nearer running rail.   The line to Coombe Junction and Looe passing beneath the viaduct can just be made out below the white fence posts.

5. As it only has eight coaches, this up evening train calling at Liskeard must be double headed to reduce line occupation. The engines are no. 7022 *Cromwells Castle* and 4908 *Broome Hall*, both with smoke and steam to spare.

6. The small shelter at the extreme left was for the postman in wet weather, as he watched over the picking up of bags by the up Mail. The gradient down from Liskeard station on the right is shown by the level siding on the left, and no. 7925 *Westol Hall* is already coasting down the 1 in 60 to Moorswater viaduct.

7. The gradient flattend out across the viaduct before the climb at 1 in 60 westwards towards Doublebois. The train is in the down "Royal Duchy", 1.30pm Paddington to Penzance. Below it is Moorswater depot, once the headquarters of the Liskeard & Caradon Railway (behind the camera, and closed in 1917) and the Liskeard & Looe. Coombe Junction, where the connection from Liskeard on the main line is made, is out of sight beyond the viaduct.

8. Quite why the Cornwall Railway provided a station at Doublebois is not obvious, because there was no village close by. Maybe the existance of Doublebois House gives a clue: was its owner once a substantial supporter? It didn't help in 1964 when the station closed. The significant distance between the track upon which no. 6860 *Aberporth Grange* is running with a down train, and the up line nearer the camera, is a relic of the broad gauge.

9. *Westol Hall* again, this time entering the trim surroundings of Bodmin Road (now Bodmin Parkway) station with a down train. In the background is the branch train for Bodmin General, properly equipped with a side destination board on its GWR carriages.

10. Looking west off the end of the platform at Bodmin Road we see no. 4928 *Gatacre Hall* at grips with the 1 in 74 up from Lostwithiel. The line on the left going into the goods shed is level, which gives some idea of the drag on the engine, made heavier by the reverse curve.

11. The frequent curvature of the Cornwall Railway main line prevented express drivers from taking advantage of the downhill stretches into a river valley to rush the succeeding climb out of it. The driver of no. 7031 *Cromwells Castle* has shut off steam approaching Lostwithiel with the up "Cornish Riviera Express", its gleaming carriages contrasting with the filthy engine. There are also palm trees and GWR platform seats to be admired.

13. Par is the junction for the Newquay line and on 16th August 1959 one of the post-war GWR "County" class, no. 1007 *County of Brecknock*, has detached the Newquay portion and is now continuing westwards with the 9.30am Paddington to Falmouth. The Newquay branch platform is to the left of the 1879 signal box which was still standing in 1993.

12. At the other end of Lostwithiel station there is a level crossing, over the goods yard sidings as well as the main line. Before gates operated from the signal box were introduced in 1874, the man working the manual gates was warned of an approaching train by the station staff using a wooden rattle. To the right of no. 5148 is the down refuge siding, used at busy times to shunt a slow goods, like this one, out of the way of a following passenger train.

14. The LNER carriages behind no. 4976 *Warfield Hall* suggest this up train at St. Austell is bound for northern England, or even Scotland, if it is the 12 noon Penzance to Manchester and Glasgow. There are certainly plenty of passengers with suitcases on the platform in 1959, when the station was still lit by gas.

15. The starting signal is on a wooden post at the end of St. Austell down platform, its arm not in the usual steeply inclined GWR position (see picture 27) as no. 6828 *Trellech Grange* passes an up goods working. Passengers who have alighted may include some for Treviscoe and St. Dennis, who will continue their journey by the bus waiting in the goods yard.

16. Grampound Road, a victim of the 1964 closure drive, was still well kept five years earlier. It stood at the summit of severe gradients from both directions, which accounts for the effort being displayed by no. 4095 *Harlech Castle* as it passes with a down parcels train.

17. Brunel's wooden Carvedras Viaduct over the River Kenwyn at the east end of Truro station was replaced in 1902, though its stone piers remained, covered in ivy, beside the new bridge. Until 1898 there was a tin smelting works at this sylvan spot, almost under the viaduct. In the distance is the foot of the 1 in 70 gradient from Buckshead Tunnel, down which has come no. 6823 *Oakley Grange* with the 9.10am Plymouth to Penzance semi-fast service.

18. Turning right round immediately after the previous scene, the observer would see the up "Cornish Riviera Express" pulling out bound for Par, Plymouth and Paddington. One of the few Cornish services at this date to be formed of BR standard stock, the well cleaned and roof-boarded train was in the charge of no. 5066 *Sir Felix Pole*, leaving a threatening sky behind.

19. Moving now to the west end of Truro station, another up train appears, double headed by no. 1018 *County of Leicester* and an unidentified Hall class 4-6-0. They have just emerged from the short Highertown Tunnel and are passing the engine shed, which is in the process of being rebuilt.

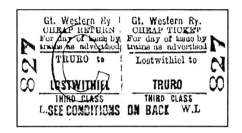

20. The original Cornwall Railway main line from Plymouth straight to Falmouth is on the right, the line connecting to the West Cornwall Railway curving away sharply here at Penwithers Junction. No. 1002 *County of Berks* is at the head of a down train, looking very powerful from this viewpoint. Alas, none of these handsome engines was preserved.

21. This unusual train, carrying the express headcode and hauled by a pair of 2-6-2 tanks with no. 5562 in the lead, is on the main line between Chacewater and Penwithers Junction. It is the Saturdays only 8.15am from Perranporth to Paddington, very much a holiday-makers train and requiring two engines for the severe gradients of the run from Perranporth. I believe it ran via Chacewater rather than the Newquay - Par line because the latter was too busy on summer Saturdays. The 2-6-2 tanks will be replaced at Truro.

22. An up loop platorm at Chacewater for Newquay branch trains was added to the layout in 1912. Although one of the original stations of the West Cornwall Railway, Chacewater closed in 1964, eighteen months after the demise of the branch to Newquay. In 1959 no. 6828 *Trellech Grange* is just leaving the up main platform with the 7.55am Penzance - Truro stopping train.

23. Despite the almost total decline of mining in West Cornwall, in the 1950s there still seemed to be a useful number of local goods trains like this up service hauled by no. 4508 at Scorrier. A close look at the opposite platform shows how its original stone block face has been made higher for modern trains by several courses of brickwork. Scorrier, which closed in 1964, was still lit by oil five years earlier. Notice the means provided for the porter to reach the lamps when they needed attention.

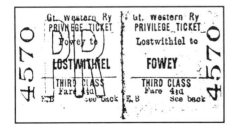

24. Behind this up train entering Redruth is the mass of Carn Brea from which, a century earlier, an observer would have seen scores of working mine shafts. The hill is crowned by a sham castle and the de Dunstanville monument. Beside this grandeur no. 5934 *Kneller Hall* seems rather mundane.

25. Carn Brea was once called Pool and was the headquarters of the Hayle Railway, Carn Brea Yard being behind no. 6319 which is arriving from Redruth. The platforms are devoid of any form of lighting and the seat is of the first GWR standard. Carn Brea closed in 1961 before the majority of the main line stations that were shut. Copper and tin mines of great importance working the Dolcoath Main Lode once completely surrounded the railway here, the engine house and stepped stack of the long-closed Carn Brea mine still standing on the right in 1959.

26. The Castle class was the heaviest GWR 4-6-0 allowed in Cornwall, and the fact that no. 5020 *Trematon Castle* is only working a stopping train must be in order to get it to Penzance for something more important. The platforms here at Camborne were of unequal length so this picture can show part of the goods shed and two types of bulk milk transport used in 1959. Next to the six-wheeled milk tank we can just see one of the demountable (road) variety on its flat wagon.

27. Still at Camborne, no. 6938 *Cornden Hall* is seen coming up the 1 in 60 gradient from the west, by which in 1852 the original Hayle Railway 1 in 22 incline at Penponds (behind the trees in the distance) was avoided when the West Cornwall Railway took over. The Hayle Railway passed through the goods yard on the level, where more milk tanks awaited filling.

28. Because of the addition in 1887 of a platform on the left for Helston branch trains, the level crossing at the east end of Gwinear Road station was of unusual width with very long gates. The main line curves sharply here so the up line signals would be very bad for sighting if they were at the end of the platform. Instead they are on the footbridge, over the down line.

The branch starting signal is also on the "wrong" side. No. 1007 *County of Brecknock* has called with an up train while the usual 2-6-2 tank waits with the branch train at its own platform. All this activity ceased in 1964 with the mass station closures in Corwall.

29. This is a scene of Cornish industrial history. The Hayle Railway of 1837 began directly below the viaduct, alongside the buildings of Harvey's great Hayle Foundry whence came so many famous pumping engines for the mines. When the West Cornwall Railway was built in 1852 it crossed the inner end of the harbour by a wooden viaduct on piers, wooden except for one. This actually stood inside the foundry building and was of stone because of the fire risk. The train is crossing the replacement stone viaduct of 1886, but the connection on the right going down to Hayle wharves (see picture 64) dates from 1852.

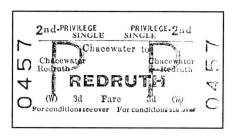

30. In this view of Hayle Viaduct, Chapel Road is in the foreground, the quayside line of Hayle Railway is behind the wall above the cars, and the Hayle Foundry is off to the left. There is also some vintage transport on view, including no. 6832 *Brockton Garage* on a down train.

31. A wooden post signal and GWR platform trolleys galore adorn the down platform as no. 6849 *Walton Grange* calls with the 7.30am Penzance to Manchester. Even at this early hour there was a connection from St. Ives. The seat by the running-in board is certainly not GWR standard. Did it date from Cornwall Railway days?

→

32. Marazion was the last station before Penzance, prior to the closure of the former in 1964. On 13th August 1959 the up "Cornishman" (10.30am Penzance - Wolverhampton) worked by no. 1002 *County of Berks* passes a goods yard which was a hive of activity in the spring with early vegetables being loaded for big city markets. The platform seat is of the post-1934 design, with an eccentric painting scheme to its legs.

→

33. Journey's end. Only a short one in this case, for this is the 6.50am from Plymouth arriving at Penzance. *County of Brecknock* is the engine, passing the station pilot, an 0-6-0 pannier tank, with a "Grange" class 4-6-0 in the distance.

34. Journey's beginning. The train at platform 1 is the "Cornish Riviera Express" for Paddington, which is **not** 326½ miles away, because the milepost distances were measured via the original route through Bristol and this train has 20 miles less to go. This picture shows how traffic at Penzance outgrew the roofed portion of the terminus as rebuilt in 1880.

GREAT WESTERN BRANCHES SOUTH OF
THE MAIN LINE

Remembering the slaughter which has taken place elsewhere, it must be said that the branch lines of Cornwall have been let off lightly. Three of the four south of the main line still carry trains. All of them had quite different origins, though the minerals which once sustained the Cornish economy played a part in three of them.

Coming west, the first to be depicted is the Liskeard & Looe line. In the last century tin, copper and granite were all worked in the country north of Liskeard, and getting them to navigable water produced first a canal southward from Moorswater west of Liskeard. A railway to the mining area around Caradon followed in 1844, which was extended south to Looe in 1860 because the canal could not deal with the traffic needs of the mines and quarries. In 1879 the line began to carry passengers, though by then the best years of the Caradon mines were over. All this was independent of the GWR striding loftily on its viaduct above the little local line at Moorswater. In 1901 the mineral railway realised its future lay with passengers to Looe rather than tin and copper, and it opened an almost circular link from Coombe Junction south of Moorswater to the Great Western's Liskeard station. The whole lot was taken over by the GWR in 1909. The lines north of Moorswater died in 1917 but the Looe passenger service survives, albeit to a terminus at Looe which provides only the barest facilities for passengers.

The link between Lostwithiel and Fowey was built in 1869 to provide an alternative route for china clay being loaded on board ships at Fowey, in competition with the Cornwall Minerals Railway's route from St. Blazey. It did not flourish, and saw its last broad gauge trains in 1880. The GWR revived it as a standard gauge line in 1895; with increasing output of china clay from the country north of St. Austell, both routes were busy. The GWR (which by then owned the former CMR) provided impressive equipment for loading the clay onto ships at Carne Point north of Fowey in 1908, and the line still carries clay via Lostwithiel. The Fowey passenger service was a victim of the "Beeching" cuts in 1965. As the St. Blazey - Fowey line was an extension of the branches north of the main line, its story is in the next chapter.

In pre-steamship days Falmouth was a place of great importance, being the first well-sheltered roadstead of any size encountered by sailing vessels coming up the Channel from all over the world. "Call at Falmouth for orders" was a sailing instruction carried by thousand of skippers over several centuries. In addition, Falmouth was a packet port until 1844, whence sailed passenger ships for America and many other places. In those days it was often quicker to come to Falmouth by land from the rest of Southern England, rather than by sea. Few people realised that steam shipping would begin the decline of Falmouth's glory, most certainly not the promoters of the Cornwall Railway, for their main line was intended to run from Plymouth to Falmouth. It didn't quite work out like that. For a start they ran out of money, much of what they had being swallowed by the heroic task of bridging the Tamar at Saltash. The existence of the West Cornwall Railway between Truro and Penzance made them reappraise their undertaking in terms of being part of a through route to the far west. So although the CR reached Truro in 1859, Falmouth did not get its rails until 1863. The port did not die suddenly; there were still many cargoes which navigated the oceans under sail, and Falmouth also developed a ship repairing business. Never so dependent on the tourist and the holidaymaker as other places on Cornwall's south coast, it is a line virtually without staffed stations.

The Helston branch story is in some ways a sad one. The Helston peninsula once had mines of fabulous wealth, but successive declines in the price of copper killed them despite several very expensive attempts to reopen. When the standard gauge line from Gwinear Road was opened in 1887, mineral traffic was largely in the minds of those who dreamed of rich veins still unworked below the dark flooded tunnels of abandoned mines. By the twentieth century the GWR, who worked the line, was actively promoting Cornwall for tourism and in this the branch played an interesting part. Helston was at one end of a bone-shaking bus service which from 1903 connected with the spectacular scenery of the

Lizard peninsula. Between the two world wars tourist traffic grew steadily, probably reaching is peak in the 1950s before mass car owning and package holidays brought it low. Passenger trains were withdrawn in 1962 and the line was lifted after complete closure in 1967.

Leaving aside special traffic, the branches south of the main line were, in the 1950s, mostly worked by the popular GWR 2-6-2 tanks of the 45XX and 55XX types, with two coaches in winter building up to four or more in the summer holidays. The same engines were quite suited to working goods traffic, so they appear in almost every picture in this chapter. Happily a number of them have escaped scrapping and are preserved for our delight.

35. The platform at Liskeard for trains from Looe is at an angle to the main line, and here it receives a typical branch train in the last years of steam. Apart from the livery of engine and carriages the scene is pure GWR.

36. With the south side of Moorswater Viaduct as a backcloth, Coombe Junction is still
the place of reversal for every train on the Looe
branch. Having come down the bank from
Liskeard bunker first, no. 4565 has run round
its train and now stands ready for the 7 mile
trip to Looe. The stack is a typical Cornish
design, of stone in its lower portion with a brick
top.

37. In 1959 Moorswater Depot dealt with
china clay traffic, and here a short train of it,
sheeted in open wagons, has just passed
Coombe Junction signal box on its way to Liskeard. The 2-6-2 tanks were just as much at
home on a task such as this as on the more
frequently photographed passenger trains,
though the headcode is novel.

38. This train from Liskeard is at the foot of the 1901 connection from the main line and is approaching the physical junction at Coombe. As the gradient was nearly all down at 1 in 40 it has coasted most of the way. The line to Looe going to the right replaced a canal and was virtually level.

39. Coombe Junction served the hamlet of Lamellion nearby but at St. Keyne there was only a mill, even the ancient well being some distance away. Nevertheless on 18th August 1959 there were passengers for Looe and we must hope that poor roads in the upper part of the Looe river valley will keep St. Keyne in business for many years to come.

40. The permanent way gang responsible for the branch was given personal transport in the shape of a petrol driven 4-wheeled trolley so it didn't have to depend on the kindness of engine crews to get about their area. Officially this was known as the Motor Trolley System of Maintenance. At Causeland Halt the trolley has been moved clear of the running lines onto a short track of its own, an activity coordinated with the signalman at Coombe by means of an occupation key instrument in the box alongside.

41. Traffic on the branch did not consist only of trains between Liskeard and Looe. This is a summer's day excursion from Exeter to Looe, here passing the (very basic) Sandplace Halt without stopping.

42. This Looe station is no more, its place having been taken by a basic concrete structure beyond where the signal stands. The Looe river is wide and tidal here but the tracks in the foreground no longer lead to riverside quays where once granite from the Cheesewring was loaded for shipment.

43. This is the train movement which preceded the one shown in picture 11. It has just arrived at Lostwithiel after a 5-mile run from Fowey, 15 minutes being allowed. This branch was the only one hereabouts where pull and push working was in use, the engines being slightly more modern 2-6-2 tanks of the 4575 series transferred from South Wales. The large stone building behind is a relic of the days when Lostwithiel was the enginering head-quarters of the Cornwall Railway.

44. The Fowey branch has but one intermediate halt, at Golant beside the river, and that is of modern concrete construction. China clay trains still pass Golant, and no. 5572 has been preserved, though it doesn't run to Fowey any more.

45. Fowey station is seen here from the east, with the branch train just arrived from Lost-withiel. Ahead of it, the tracks lead to Par but are only used for goods trains. The building on the extreme left was the original Cornwall Minerals Railway station and the line on the left originally served an engine shed. Fowey's passenger service ended in 1965, the signal box closing in 1968 with the direct line from Par.

46. As the branch train approaches we can see that the route to Falmouth was originally intended to be the main line, losing that status when the Cornwall and West Cornwall Railways were joined together at Penwithers Junction. In the background the view is clear right through Highertown tunnel towards Truro station. The line going off on the right leads to Newham goods station, the West Cornwall railway terminus in Truro before the Cornwall Railway arrived from Plymouth. Until 1893 the Newham line came straight off the WCR line from Penzance, crossing the Falmouth branch on the level.

47. This picture of a Falmouth train at Per-ranwell shows how the site in a cutting is very restricted for space. To make the most of what there is, the signal box was built with a siding running beneath it, giving the photographer his elevated viewpoint of the gardens beside the up platform and the neat Cornwall Railway buildings.

48.   As no.5562 departs we can observe the unusual signal box, probably built in the 1890s. The running-in board which is mounted on old rails carries the station name in the older GWR style.

49.   Penryn signal box at the Falmouth end of the down platform was more modern than Perranwell's. It has windows with large panes and the so-called "rocket" ventilators. The fireman on no.9476 has hung the Falmouth - Penryn staff on the projecting "horn" in the background and just caught the Penryn - Perranwell staff by its attached ring. A second ago it was sticking out at an angle from the top of the wooden post (with lamp) at the bottom of the ramp, where the signalman had placed it a few minutes before.

50.   Penmere Platform was opened in July 1925 as Falmouth grew, housing of the period being visible on top of the bank. There was no passing loop here, only a long headshunt for the Admiralty sidings behind the camera which were laid down in 1940. By 1959 the headshunt was used for storing wagons. Among the more modern tank engines in Cornwall (some of the 2-6-2 tanks dated back to 1907) was the 9400 class 0-6-0 pannier variety. No.9476 was built for BR by Stephensons in 1952.

51. Falmouth's resurgence after its decline as a packet port dated from 1860, with the opening of new docks. The railway arrived belatedly in 1863 and down the years the sheltered deep water anchorage and a developing trade in ship repairing have kept it from becoming moribund. Holiday makers began to come in the 1870s and this traffic reached its peak between the wars. Ships and tourists between them have kept the railway open. The modern platform awnings in this 1959 view replaced a Brunellian all-over roof but, alas, today there only remains a single unstaffed platform.

52. Praze was the first station down the Helston branch from Gwinear Road and this picture shows the arrival of the train from Helston, carrying a party of schoolchildren who have spent the day there. The other track was once a running loop but latterly was disconnected at the Helston end. The ground frame was placed in the small building on the right.

53. Somewhat unusually for a wayside station, Praze possessed a water tank and crane, probably provided because there seemed to be no facility for engines to take water at Gwinear Road. This down goods train includes two hopper wagons for stone traffic which developed at Helston in the final years of the branch.

54. Nancegollen had extensive sidings for goods traffic, especially early flowers, potatoes and broccoli in season. The passenger station was rebuilt in 1937 and given a second platform, allowing passenger workings to cross where previously this facility was only available for goods trains. As no.4570 calls with an up train, the photographer shelters from the downpour under the substantial awning attached to the main station building, while cattle trucks wait in the siding.

55. The Helston branch ganger also had the use of a trolley, here pushed into a weedy siding by the loading bank. The 10.50am from Gwinear Road obscures the engine shed as it arrives, with the signalman on hand to collect the single line staff. Although the box was built by the Helston Railway Co. (which the GWR bought in 1898), it appears in very early photographs and was probably constructed in GWR style in 1887 or soon after.

56. Helston arrival. The train seen in the previous picture having come to a stop, before the engine was uncoupled prior to running round the carriages there was a pause. This enabled the fireman (distinguished from other males in the picture by his long trousers) to visit the Refreshment Room. Behind the camera the rails continued to their most southerly point in Great Britain : Helston carriage shed.

57. Helston departure. On Thursday 13th August 1959 there was no throng of passengers on the platform joining the 1.15pm to Gwinear Road. Today the station buildings have all gone and only the goods shed on the left remains. The original dream of Helston being a passing station on a line to the beauties of the Lizard peninsula remained a dream, though the station was laid out for through running, just in case. The two platform trolleys are GWR standard type.

Great Western Branches north of the Main Line

St. Ives, with its superb light and wide inviting sands, has long been attractive to artists and holidaymakers. Yet even here there was mining, admittedly in terminal decline when the branch from St. Erth was opened in 1877. It was the very last piece of the broad gauge ever built. Although there was once some freight traffic between the main line and Lelant Quay, for most of its life the St. Ives branch has been mainly concerned with passengers. Threatened by the Beeching axe in the 1960s, reprieved in the 1970s, and given a new station at Lelant Saltings in 1978, the branch still carries passengers beside the beautiful expanse of St. Ives Bay.

Hayle developed considerably as a port in the eighteenth century and by 1800 both a major copper smelting works and a sizable foundry had been established. When, under the impact of the mines' need for transport, a railway was created, it started beside the Hayle quays. Passing through a major tin and copper mining area, the Hayle Railway divided at its eastern end, sending a branch north to the coast at Portreath (north of Redruth), and also going on eastwards to Redruth. Its two inclines were bypassed when it became part of the West Cornwall Railway, cutting off the parts around Hayle harbour. A connection down to them was provided from the new main line immediately west of Hayle station and this remained in use, latterly as a private siding, until 1983. At the other end of the Hayle Railway, Portreath died as a port with the mines which called it into existence, their pumping engines stopped and no longer demanding coal in huge amounts. The track was lifted in the late 1930s but the formation of the impressive 1 in 7 incline down to the harbour remains. It would be hard to destroy.

Moving east along the main line we come to Chacewater, and now the story gets complicated. In fact it began not here but further east still, at Fowey on the south coast. There in 1842 lived Joseph Thomas Treffry, who owned much land away to the north-west beyond St. Blazey in the next valley. In 1842 he built a tramway from his moorland holdings round about "the Bugle Inn at Molinnis", descending by an incline to the river at Ponts Mill, and a canal thence to the sea at Par.

Two years later he began another tramway from Newquay on the north coast eastwards to St. Dennis, but short of the Bugle terminus of his first line. This opened in 1849. Although Treffry died the following year his successors built a new branch south from Newquay to serve the great East Wheal Rose lead mine. Twenty years after Treffry's death, W.R. Roebuck appeared on the scene and created the Cornwall Minerals Railway out of Treffry's lines. He completed the Newquay - Par link (St. Dennis - Bugle), took over various lines in the developing china clay district south of St. Dennis, and built a line in the Luxulyan valley to bypass the Carmears incline down to Ponts Mill. The canal thence to Par had been replaced by a railway, which was continued through the ridge to Fowey to join the Lostwithiel - Fowey Railway at Carne Point. All this was opened (with locomotives replacing horses) in 1874, and there matters rested until the LSWR push into Cornwall to connect with its Bodmin & Wadebridge outpost. The South Western finally linked up with the B&W in 1895 and extended from Wadebridge to Padstow in 1899. This gave the GWR - which by then owned the Cornwall Minerals Railway - a fright, for the LSWR was looking longingly at Newquay and the developing holiday coast round that popular resort. The GWR proposal for a near-direct line from Truro to Newquay had been defeated by local opposition which favoured the LSWR, as a competitor to the somewhat monopolistic GWR. It was resurrected in the shape of a roundabout line from Chacewater through Perranporth to Newquay. Part of it took over Treffry's East Wheal Rose line between Shepherds and Newquay. The new route passed through some pretty quiet country; most of the stops on it were halts provided soon after the opening in 1903, but it met a local need. On summer Saturdays in the 1950s it became quite busy with holidaymakers and even boasted a through train to Paddington. But the countryside was too sparsely populated and, even with minimal station costs, the Chacewater-Newquay line could not survive in the economic climate of the 1960s, closing in 1963. Latterly most of its local trains had continued over the main line to

Truro.

Treffry's original route to Bugle and Newquay survives, realigned in the Luxulyan valley by the CMR. Nowadays, a single diesel railcar meets most of its passengers' needs, but there is still useful traffic in china clay. Originally its south end passed beneath the Cornwall Railway main line but a connection between the two was made by the St. Blazey - Par loop in 1879. This is how trains reach the line up the Luxulyan valley today. The steeply graded portion between St. Blazey (south of Ponts Mill) and Fowey has been lifted and is today a private road, including Pinnock tunnel. The GWR branches in Cornwall were all interesting, and some were picturesque, but for me Squire Treffry's railway is the best.

Lastly I must mention Bodmin, which saw its first trains in 1834 when the Bodmin &

Wadebridge opened. Although Bodmin was the county town, the hard-up Cornwall Railway could not afford £11,000 to build a branch to it, so Bodmin's transport link with the rest of England remained a horse bus to Bodmin Road station on the GWR main line. However, in 1887 LSWR ambitions to connect with its isolated outpost at Wadebridge frightened the GWR into action and a three mile branch from the main line to Bodmin itself was opened. The following year an extension to Boscarne Junction on the B&W gave the GWR access to the china clay and granite traffic from Wenford Bridge. BR renamed the GWR station Bodmin General in 1949, but passenger services ceased in 1967. China clay trains continued until 1983 and ten years later the activities of the Bodmin & Wenford Railway ensure that steam is still seen at Bodmin.

58. Would today's environment of Health & Safety consciousness allow the casually dangerous pose of the St. Ives branch fireman on no.4571 ? And what of the St. Erth signalman in his braces, who has just come within arm's length of a moving train as he caught the hoop with the single line tablet attached ? In 1959, as for many years previously, such actions were all in a day's work.

59. Although there had once been a rail-connected quay beside the Hayle river at Lelant on the St. Ives branch, and prospering mines too, by 1959 all the goods traffic could be handled by a daily mixed train. No.4566 is still running in preservation but here it works the 8.00am from St. Erth to St. Ives, slowing for its first stop at Lelant. Luckily for the photographer the tide was out.

60. Later in the morning no.4566 returned, stopping again at Lelant which has a wooden building on a concrete raft because the ground here is sand. The track to the quay was between the present line and the shore, just out of sight to the right. Today there is an additional station at Lelant Saltings, half way between here and St. Erth, and a "park & ride" arrangement for those who want to avoid the traffic congestion at St. Ives.

61. Once the Hayle estuary is left behind the branch rises to a shelf above the shore with cuttings, embankments and the Carbis Viaduct, here being crossed by an up train. The driver of no. 4566 has shut the regulator to stop at Carbis Bay station, which is behind the camera, and the fireman has put the injector on to try to stop the engine blowing off after the effort of the climb from St. Ives.

62. A fine summer day has brought the visitors out in force and the branch trains have been strengthened to five coaches. This service is just leaving the terminus and is passing in front of the goods shed before heading up the bank to Carbis Bay, which includes a gradient of 1 in 44. Quite what happened to the goods trucks in picture 59 is a mystery, as the intermediate stations had no sidings and the St. Ives goods shed line was occupied by a camping coach on 14th August 1959.

LOSTWITHIEL and FOWEY

WEEK DAYS ONLY—(Second class only)

Miles		am	am		am	am E		am S		pm S	pm E	pm S			pm	pm S			pm S	pm			pm S
	Lostwithiel .. .. dep	7 58	8 20	..	9 5	1015	..	1020	..	1210	1225	1 5	..	2 25	3 15	..	4 55	5	..	6 10	7 0	..	8 10
3¾	Golant Halt	7 14	3 29	..	9 14	1024	..	1029	..	1219	1234	1 14	..	2 34	3 24	..	4 14	5 14	..	6 19	7 9	..	8 19
5½	Fowey .. .. arr	7 20	8 35	..	9 20	1030	..	1035	..	1225	1240	1 20	..	2 40	3 30	..	4 20	5 20	..	6 25	7 15	..	8 25

Miles		am S	am E	am		am E	am S		am S	am E		pm S	pm S	pm E	pm S	pm E	pm S		pm	pm		pm S	pm S
	Fowey .. .. dep	7 25	7 30	8 40	..	9 30	9 45	..	1135	1155	..	1235	1 35	45	3 35	4 30	4 35	..	5 35	6 30	..	7 25	9 5
1¾	Golant Halt	7 30	7 35	9 45	..	9 35	9 50	..	1140	12 0	..	1240	1 40	1 50	3 40	4 35	4 40	..	5 40	6 35	..	7 30	9 10
5½	Lostwithiel .. .. arr	7 40	7 45	8 55	..	9 45	10 0	..	1150	1210	..	1250	1 50	2 0	3 50	4 45	4 50	..	5 50	6 45	..	7 40	9 20

E Except Saturdays   S Saturdays only

63. The platform, run-round loop, and station buildings at St. Ives were all swept away by 1971 and the site is now a car park. The present basic platform is near the site of the signal box visible above the light engine waiting to back onto the service which has just arrived. At least the trains still run.

64. When the Hayle Railway was modernised as the West Cornwall Railway, its important riverside lines at Hayle would have been cut off, so a branch was made from the new line towards Penzance, down to the drawbridge over Copperhouse Creek : see picture 29. The difference in level needed a gradient of 1 in 30 at the foot of which was the world's first sand drag. Pannier tank no. 9748 is just crossing the bridge before climbing to the main line. The original course of the Hayle Railway turned right on the far side of the bridge, heading for the Angarrack incline and Redruth. The Ministry of Labour and National Service on the left was once Hayle Custom House.

65. Whereas Hayle port retained rail access in 1959, one of the Hayle Railway's other terminals, at Portreath harbour north of Redruth lost its tracks in 1936. This is a view up the 1 in 7 double track incline which led down to the small port. Its decline accompanied that of Cornish copper and tin mining which first called it into existence. Although the port was privately owned, the rail connection was part of the Hayle Railway.

66. The improvements to the Cornwall main line over the years included doubling its original single track as well as rebuilding the viaducts. As traffic grew it seemed sensible to provide an independent single line on the up side from Blackwater Junction (where the Newquay line came in) to Chacewater station. This was done in 1924 and this train off the branch is running on it, past the goods yard at Chacewater. It will call at the up loop platform (see picture 22) before going on to end its journey at Truro.

67. The first halt along the Newquay branch was called Mount Hawke, in the middle of nowhere where a by-road crossed the line. The hamlet of Mount Hawke was about a mile away to the west. As we shall see, the amenities provided at the many halts by the GWR were of their standard basic variety.

68. St. Agnes station was also a fair distance from the place of that name - Goonbell was slightly nearer - but at least there **was** a place for the station to serve. Once it had been the centre of an important mining district but by the time the railway came in 1903 that activity was long past its best. Between the wars St. Agnes prospered with holidaymakers and in 1937 the GWR made the single platform into an island one, thereby allowing passenger trains to cross one another on the single line. The original Edwardian station buildings were still occupied in 1993.

69. Passengers on trains between St. Agnes and Perranporth enjoyed fine views over the countryside round about Goonbell, with glimpses of the sea. This is the 4.35pm from Newquay to Chacewater, one of the few services which did not run through to Truro. The engine with the usual three coach weekday set is no.5562.

TRURO, CHACEWATER, PERRANPORTH and NEWQUAY
(Second class only except where otherwise shewn)

Miles		Week Days am	am	am	am E	am S	am T	pm	pm	pm P	pm	pm E	pm S	pm ST	pm ET	pm S	Sundays am	am	am T	am	pm	pm	pm	pm T	pm T
—	**Truro** .. dep	6F 0	7F10	8H45	10 8	1010	1140	1H15	2J48	3 45	4L15	5H43	6 15	7 42	750	910	845	9 25	1130	1155	151	.	440	542	725
5	**Chacewater**	6 16	7 26	9 15	1020	1023	1154	1 35	2 58	3 55	4 39	5 58	6 25	8 0	810	922	...	9 37	1144	12 6	2 2	...	451	553	736
6¾	Mount Hawke Halt	6 21	7 31	9 20	..	..	1159	1 40	3 3	..	4 44	6 3	6 30	8 5	815	927	.	9 42	1149	1211	2 8	.	456	558	741
8½	St. Agnes	6 26	7 36	9 25	1028	1030	12 4	1 45	3 8	4 5	4 49	6 8	6 40	8 10	820	932	...	9 47	1154	1216	214	...	5 1	6 4	746
9	Goonbell Halt	6 29	7 39	9 28	..	..	12 7	1 48	3 11	..	4 52	6 11	6 44	8 13	823	935	.	9 50	1157	1219	217	.	5 4	6 7	749
10¾	Mithian Halt	6 34	7 44	9 33	....	....	1212	1 53	3 16	....	4 57	6 16	6 49	8 18	828	940	...	9 55	12 2	1224	222	...	5 9	612	754
13	Perranporth Beach Halt ..	6 39	7 49	9 38	1038	1040	1218	1 59	3 21	..	5 2	6 21	6 55	8 22	832	945	.	10 0	12 7	1229	227	.	513	617	759
13¼	**Perranporth**	6 41	8B 2	9 41	1040	1044	1221	2 4	3 23	4 20	5 5	6 24	6 57	8 24	834	948	912	10 2	12 9	1230	230	435	515	620	8 1
15¾	Goonhavern Halt	6 49	8 10	9 49	..	..	1230	2 12	3 31	..	5 14	6 33	7 5	8 32	842	.	.	1010	1216	..	237	442	523	628	8 9
17¾	Shepherds	6 56	8 17	9 56	1052	....	1236	2 19	3 39	....	5 20	6 40	7 11	8 39	848	...	...	1018	1223	....	244	449	530	637	816
19	Mitchell and Newlyn Halt.	6 59	8 20	10 0	..	..	1240	2 22	3 43	..	5 24	6 43	7 15	8 43	851	.	.	1022	1226	..	248	453	534	641	821
21	Trewerry and Trerice Halt.	7 4	8 25	10 5	....	....	1245	2 27	3 48	....	5 29	6 48	7 20	8 49	856	...	...	1027	1231	....	253	458	539	646	826
23¾	**Newquay** .. .. .. arr	7 12	8 32	1015	11 6	..	1255	2 35	3 55	..	5 36	6 56	7 29	8 55	9 5	.	940	1035	1239	..	3 0	5 5	547	655	835

Miles		Week Days am	am K	am	am S	am ET	am	pm	pm S	pm E	pm	pm	pm E	pm S	pm S	Sundays am	am T	pm	pm	pm	pm T	pm T	pm
—	**Newquay** .. .. .. dep	7 20	..	9 12	..	11 0	1150	1 35	2 55	3 20	4 35	5 52	7 10	7 55	9 15	10 0	1050	..	1 30	4 0	620	8 0	8 50
2¾	Trewerry and Trerice Halt.	7 27	....	9 19	....	....	1157	1 42	3 2	3 27	4 43	5 59	7 17	8 2	9 21	10 6	....	....	1 37	4 6	626	8 6	8 56
4¾	Mitchell and Newlyn Halt.	7 33	..	9 24	..	..	12 3	1 48	3 8	3 33	4 49	6 5	7 23	8 7	9 27	10 12	..	..	1 43	412	633	812	9 2
6	Shepherds	7 37	....	9 28	....	1114	12 7	1 53	3 12	3 38	4 53	6 9	7 27	8 11	9 32	10 17	11 3	....	1 47	417	637	817	9 7
8	Goonhavern Halt	7 43	..	9 33	..	1120	1212	1 58	3 17	3 43	4 59	6 14	7 33	8 16	9 37	10 22	..	..	1 52	422	642	822	9 12
10½	**Perranporth**	7 50	8 15	9 39	11 0	1125	1220	2 4	3 24	3 49	5 5	6 23	7 38	8 25	9 43	10 28	1116	1 10	1 58	428	649	828	9 18
10¾	Perranporth Beach Halt ..	7 51	..	9 41	11 2	1127	1222	2 5	3 25	3 51	5 7	6 25	7 41	8 26	9 47	10 30	..	1 11	2 0	.	651	830	9 20
13	Mithian Halt	7 58	....	9 48	....	....	1229	2 12	3 32	3 58	5 14	6 32	7 48	8 33	....	10 37	....	1 18	2 7	...	658	837	9 27
14¾	Goonbell Halt	8 4	..	9 54	..	..	1235	2 18	3 38	4 4	5 20	6 38	7 54	8 39	..	10 43	..	1 24	2 13	.	7 4	843	9 33
15¼	St. Agnes	8 7	8 28	9 57	1114	1139	1238	2 21	3 42	4 7	5 23	6 42	7 57	8 42	9 58	10 46	1130	1 27	2 16	...	7 7	846	9 36
17	Mount Hawke Halt	8 11	..	10 1	..	..	1242	2 25	3 46	4 11	5 27	6 46	8 1	8 46	..	10 50	..	1 31	2 20	.	711	850	9 40
18¾	**Chacewater** ...... arr	8 18	....	10 7	1121	1148	1248	2 31	3 52	4 17	5 33	6 52	8 6	8 53	10 9	10 56	1139	1 37	2 26	...	717	856	9 46
23¾	**Truro** .. .. "	8H35	8 48	10 20	1133	12 2	1H13	2Z41	4 5	4H50	5D55	7 2	8 18	9 3	1020	11 6	1150	1 48	2 36	.	730	9 6	10 0

B Arr 7 53 am
D Change at Chacewater. On Saturdays arr 5 45 pm without changing
E Except Saturdays
F 5 minutes later on Mondays to Fridays
H Change at Chacewater
J Change at Chacewater on Saturdays
K Saturdays only. First and Second class. Through Train to London (Pad.) arr 3 55 pm (Table 81)
L Change at Chacewater. Dep 4 25 pm on Saturdays without changing
P Saturdays only and not after 29th Aug. First and Second class. Through Carriages from London (Pad.) dep 8 25 am (Table 81)
S Saturdays only
T Through Train from or to Falmouth (Table 101)
Z Change at Chacewater on Saturdays and arr Truro 3 5 pm

70. Like many of the halts on this line, Mithian was in a cutting because it adjoined an overbridge carrying the road to a nearby settlement. The normal three coach train on the branch was well filled on 14th August 1959, all windows being open to enjoy the warm day. No.5515 is waiting for the guard's green flag before coasting down the 1 in 45 to Perranporth.

71. From July 1903 until the beginning of 1905, Perranporth was the terminus of the new line from Chacewater, the final section to Newquay not yet being ready for traffic. Right from the start it was the most important station on the line with an island platform, goods shed, water column and signal box. The latter remained in use until the line closed in 1963. Notice the economical form of track leading to the goods shed on the left : only slowly moving vehicles used it.

72. At last we get a proper view of one of the standard GWR halt shelters, the so-called "pagoda hut" economically made out of corrugated iron. Sometimes they were provided in pairs, but not at Goonhavern where a train well provided with parcels accomodation approaches from Newquay. Unlike many on the branch this halt was well placed for the community it served, but no trace of it now remains.

GtWesternRy   GtWesternRy
Chacewater   Chacewater
TO
GOONHAVERN
HALT
THIRD CLASS
1/11 P Fare 1/11 P
Goonhavern   Goonhavern
FOR CONDITIONS SEE BACK. W.D

74. After a brief pause, no.5500 is on the move again. Shepherds was where the new line from Chacewater joined the Cornwall Mineral Railways 1874 extension from East Wheal Rose to the iron mines around the Treamble branch, which went off to the right just here, following the line of the low retaining wall. It was finally lifted in the 1950s. Where once there were platforms, a signal box and a camping coach (on the left), today there is just a muddy farmyard.

73. Shepherds was a passing place and a station, not a halt, with substantial buildings. The track behind no.5500 and its train rises sharply, showing that the GWR spent as little as possible on earthworks.

75. In 1849 Squire Treffry's railway grew a branch from Newquay to the great East Wheal Rose lead mine, near Newlyn East. Alas, by then the best days of the mine were over for it never recovered from a murderous flooding in 1846. Part of the mine site is on the right. When the new line all the way from Chacewater was opened Mitchell & Newlyn Halt was provided here, not situated conveniently for either settlement.

76. Despite the board on the right, the official name of the halt was Trewerry & Trerice. Unlike many of its fellows on the branch it had a level crossing rather than a bridge and there was also a siding, hence the ground frame. Its original timber platform was rebuilt in concrete, complete with a minimal shelter and a distinctly non-standard seat.

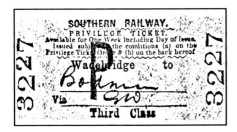

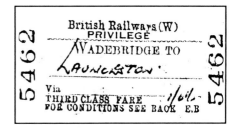

77. Newquay at last, something of a metropolis for railwaymen and passengers alike, after the remote and backwoods nature of the halts. The lengthy platforms were necessary to cope with sizeable trains of holidaymakers, the three coaches of a Chacewater train being somewhat lost in them. Platform 2 on the left became an island island platform with the addition of another face (Platform 3) in 1904/5, as traffic grew. Conversely when the diesels came the water cranes became redundant, being demolished in June 1964, five years after the date of this picture.

78. The GWR sign-producing department seems to have been in some confusion, the correct name of this place being Quintrell Downs, as the glass panel on the platform lamp confirms. Doubtless a down siding was more common. There are flowers on both sides of the line and the place looks well kept because, having a level crossing and a siding, it was regularly staffed. An 0-6-0 pannier tank makes a change from the usual 2-6-2 tank, on the 11.0am from Newquay to Par.

79.   The Par line out of Newquay carried a much heavier traffic than the Chacewater line, with a variety of engines including Hall class 4-6-0s like no. 4906 *Bradfield Hall* arriving with the 10.35am from Par. St. Columb Road had electric lights in 1959, but lost the use of its second platform six years later.   Originally it was called Halloon.

80.   While station work was being performed the photographer ran to the Newquay end of the platform and into the goods yard to capture the departure of the train.   On the opposite side of the line is the standard GWR arm and net arrangement for catching the hoop with its pouch holding the single line token.   It is illuminated by an oil lamp and bears a notice, quite illegible to the crew of the train approaching at any speed, saying "Speed not to exceed 15 miles per hour".

81. Roche also lost its crossing loop in the 1965 economy drive. The signal box is of the post-1897 type with large paned windows for good visibility. This station was first called Holy-well, then Victoria (after a nearby hamlet) until 1904, and finally Roche, a village of some importance about a mile away.

82. No. 4906 *Bradfield Hall* appears again, with the 1.45pm Newquay to Par at Bugle. The station and village seem to have got their name from the Bugle Inn at Molinnis nearby. Two china clay branches started here, to Goonbarrow and to Carbis, which is the one directly in front of the camera with a crossing gate in the distance. Beside it stand the chimneys of Wheal Hope kiln and East Goonbarrow kiln. Bugle was rebuilt as seen here with two platforms in 1931 but now only the track on the far side of the island remains.

83. Luxulyan was called Bridges until 1905, and is at the Newquay end of the 1874 deviation line avoiding the Treffry aqueduct and Carmears Wood incline. We catch *Bradfield Hall* making a second of its two round trips between Par and Newquay, and it looks as if the fire is dirty and not in good order after the climb up from St. Blazey. Unlike the ones at Quintrell Downs, these lamp standards actually have oil lamps in them.

84. Noisily the 12.20pm from Par to Newquay storms up the 1 in 37 of the deviation line through the Luxulyan valley behind no. 5195, devoid of a front numberplate. The load of six coaches was the maximum for this class here. Treffry's horse-worked route of 1842 passed over the 98ft high aqueduct on light T rails, with the water for the Carmears Wood Incline waterwheel flowing beneath the stone blocks of the tramroad. All this can still be visited, through the vegetation is more extensive than in 1959.

TRURO and FALMOUTH

Week Days

Miles		am S	am S	am E	am E	am S	am E	am S	am E	am S	am	am	am S	pm EH	pm	pm E	pm S	pm S	pm S	pm	pm S	pm EK	pm E
	Truro .. .. dep	5 35	6 38	6 38	7 28	7 47	8 8	8 25	8 50	9 10	1015	1112	1137	1210	1246	1 20	1 40	2 17	2 55	3 20	3 48	3 53	4 35
4¼	Perranwell	5 45	6 50	6 51	7 38	7 58	8 20	8 36	9 0	9 20	1025	1122	1149	1220	1256	1 30	1 51	2 27	3 8	3 30	3 58	4 3	4 45
8½	Penryn	5 55	7 0	7 3	7 47	8 9	8 29	8 47	9 10	9 30	1035	1132	1159	1230	1 6	1 40	2 0	2 37	3 20	3 40	4 7	4 12	4 55
10½	Penmere Platform	6 0	7 5	7 9	7 53	8 15	8 35	8 52	9 15	9 35	1040	1137	12 4	1235	1 11	1 45	2 5	2 42	3 25	3 45	4 12	4 18	5 0
11¾	**Falmouth** .. .. .. arr	6 5	7 12	7 15	7 58	8 20	8 40	9 0	9 20	9 40	1046	1145	1210	1242	1 18	1 50	2 11	2 59	3 30	3 50	4 20	4 25	5 5

Week Days—*continued* / **Sundays**

	pm SN	pm E	pm S	pm E	pm S	pm E	pm B	pm S	pm E	pm S	pm	Sun am	Sun am	Sun am		Sun noon H	Sun pm	Sun pm	Sun pm	Sun pm V	Sun pm H	Sun pm H	
Truro .. .. dep	4 55	5 15	6 10	6 15	6 35	7 0	7 35	8 10	8 22	9 8	9 55	7 10	8 30	10 0	..	12 0	2 0	4 0	5 14	5 50	7 45	9 15	..
Perranwell	5 8	5 25	6 20	6 25	6 46	7 10	7 45	8 21	8 32	9 17	10 4	7 22	8 41	1010	....	1210	2 10	4 10	5 24	6 0	7 55	9 26	....
Penryn	5 20	5 35	6 35	6 35	6 57	7 20	7 56	8 30	8 40	9 27	1012	7 33	8 50	1019	..	1220	2 19	4 20	5 34	6 12	8 4	9 35	..
Penmere Platform	5 25	5 40	6 40	6 40	7 2	7 25	8 1	8 35	8 45	9 33	1017	7 38	8 55	1024	....	1225	2 25	4 25	5 40	6 18	8 10	9 40	....
Falmouth .. .. .. arr	5 31	5 46	6 47	6 47	7 7	7 30	8 6	8 41	8 51	9 38	1025	7 45	9 0	1029	..	1230	2 30	4 30	5 45	6 25	8 15	9 45	..

Week Days

Miles		am S	am	am SL	am E		am ED	am S	am		am H	am S		pm S	pm E	pm S		pm	pm		pm	pm
	Falmouth .. .. dep	6 30	8 0	8 35	9 0	..	9 30	10 0	10 25	..	11 0	1125	..	1210	1220	1235	..	1 30	2 25	..	3 10	4 25
1¼	Penmere Platform	6 35	8 5	8 40	9 5	....	9 35	10 5	10 30	....	11 5	1130	....	1215	1225	1240	....	1 35	2 30	....	3 15	4 30
3¼	Penryn	6 40	8 10	8 47	9 10	..	9 43	1013	10 36	..	11 10	1136	..	1220	1230	1247	..	1 41	2 36	..	3 20	4 36
7½	Perranwell	6 50	8 19	8 56	9 20	....	9 52	1025	10 45	....	11 23	1150	....	1230	1239	1257	....	1 51	2 45	....	3 31	4 47
11¾	**Truro** .. .. arr	7 0	8 30	9 7	9 30	..	10 5	1036	10 58	..	11 35	12 0	..	1241	1250	1 8	..	2 2	2 56	..	3 41	4 58

Week Days—*continued* / **Sundays**

	pm S	pm E		pm	pm H		pm	pm		pm		Sun am	Sun am W	Sun am H		Sun pm	Sun pm		Sun pm H	Sun pm H		Sun pm	Sun pm
Falmouth .. .. dep	5 10	5 24	..	6 25	7 10	..	7 45	8 55	..	10 0	..	9 5	9 30	1050	..	1 15	2 45	..	5 5	6 45	..	8 50	10 0
Penmere Platform	5 15	5 29	....	6 30	7 15	....	7 50	9 0	....	10 5	....	9 10	9 35	1055	....	1 20	2 50	....	5 10	6 50	....	8 55	10 5
Penryn	5 21	5 35	..	6 35	7 20	..	7 55	9 5	..	1012	..	9 15	9 42	11 0	..	1 25	2 55	..	5 15	6 55	..	9 0	1010
Perranwell	5 30	5 45	....	6 47	7 29	....	8 5	9 17	....	1021	....	9 25	9 52	1110	....	1 35	3 5	....	5 25	7 5	....	9 10	1020
Truro .. .. arr	5 42	5 56	..	7 0	7 40	..	8 17	9 28	..	1033	..	9 35	10 5	1120	..	1 45	3 15	..	5 35	7 17	..	9 20	1030

B On Saturdays Through Carriages from Bristol dep 1 45 pm (Table 81)
D Through Carriages to London (Pad.) arr 4 20 pm (Table 81)
E Except Saturdays
H Through Train from or to Newquay (Table 100)
K Through Carriages from London (Pad.) dep 9 30 am (Table 81)
L Through Train to London (Pad.) arr 4 3 pm (Table 81)
N Through Carriages from London (Pad.) dep 10 35 am (Table 81)
S Saturdays only
V Through Carriages from London (Pad.) dep 10 40 am (Table 81)
W Through Carriages to London (Pad.) arr 5 10 pm (Table 81)

85. The stream in the foreground, milky white with residue from china clay working further up, is all that remains between the foot of the Luxulyan valley (at Ponts Mill) and St. Blazey, of Treffry's 1842 canal to his port of Par. No. 4930 *Hagley Hall* is working the 7.0pm Newquay to Plymouth along the railway which replaced the canal in 1855.

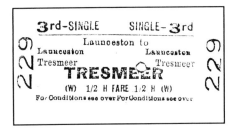

86. St. Blazey was the headquarters of the Cornwall Minerals Railway but when the connection was laid to the GWR at Par in 1879, its passenger station began to decline in importance. Closed in 1925, the platforms and buildings remained, the latter used as offices. It is still the focus of china clay traffic and provides useful siding accommodation clear of the main line. No. 4585 heads the 7.10pm from Par to Newquay through the disused platforms in August 1959.

87. In 1874 the Cornwall Minerals line from Newquay to St. Blazey and Par was extended to create a direct route onwards to Fowey with stiff gradients on either side of Pinnock Tunnel. It carried a skeleton passenger service until 1925, and an extensive china clay traffic until 1968, then becoming a private road, tunnel and all. Pannier tank no. 9655 is here making slower progress than the breeze as it struggles up the 1 in 40 from Fowey to the tunnel with empty wagons for the china clay workings further north.

88. After the direct trains from St. Blazey were withdrawn, passengers for Fowey had to travel via Lostwithiel, and this is their train at the end of its journey: see also picture 45. The signal above the coach applies to the mineral line from St. Blazey (beside the engine) and has a route indicator. This shows drivers of china clay trains their route to the wharf sidings round the corner at Carne Point, the present-day end of the line from Lostwithiel.

89. Evening sun catches the stone goods shed and the local railway lorry at Bodmin (General), but the passenger platform and GWR 4500 Class 2-6-2T No. 4552 are in shadow. This is the two coach branch train from Bodmin Road on 17th August 1959.

Southern Railway in Cornwall

There is a parallel in Cornish railway history. Just as metropolitan Paddington aimed at linking with a pioneer mineral line in the far west (the Hayle Railway), so did its rival at Waterloo. During the Railway Mania of the mid-1840s a standard gauge direct Exeter - Falmouth scheme had foundered after buying the 1834 Bodmin & Wadebridge line to get possession of its territory. The London & South Western, even then having ambitions relative to far-off Cornwall, bought the B & W from its new (and bankrupt) owners. Thereafter its affairs appeared sporadically on the agenda of the LSWR Directors, its bucolic nature providing something by way of light relief to the serious business. However as the South Western gradually progressed beyond Exeter, by 1870 the chances of getting their standard gauge rails into Cornwall brightened, and in the 1890s a great push through some lonely and difficult territory finally achieved this. Thus was the Bodmin & Wadebridge joined to Waterloo, and things down there were never the same again.

Or were they? A ride on the goods train from Wadebridge to Wenford Bridge, with the engine stopping in the middle of a wood to take water from a handy diverted stream, gave a hint of what life must have been like on the line before the link-up. The use of old 2-4-0 Well Tank engines, found nowhere else on BR, enhanced the effect, and I was but one of the steady stream of pilgrims down the years. In the 1950s local passenger trains were often worked by T9 class 4-4-0s and the dwindling band of 02 class 0-4-4 tanks, both adding to the attractions of Wadebridge as a railway centre. When finally the Well Tanks could no longer be patched up, they were briefly replaced on the Wenford Bridge line by GWR pannier tanks in 1962. These in turn gave way to diesel shunters until closure came in 1983.

I don't know who coined the phrase "The Withered Arm" to describe the Southern Railway's North Cornwall line but it was, alas, appropriate. Although the "Atlantic Coast Express" passed each way things were generally pretty quiet, as you might expect from a glance at the map of the area. By 1960 there was no service at all on Sundays. Those who went there to photograph trains really needed a car because it was almost impossible to get a picture of a train at each station in one day if you only used the railway. So it is not only reasons of space and time which restricted my coverage here of steam on the North Cornwall line. The granite and latterly china clay traffic from Wenford Bridge generally headed south via Bodmin and the GWR, while the North Cornwall's only significant mineral producer, the enormous slate quarry at Delabole, suffered as tiles became favoured for roofs from the 1920s onwards.

The Plymouth, Devonport & South Western Junction Railway from Lydford to Devonport was a satellite of the LSWR and helped it to gain access to Plymouth independent of the GWR. In Cornwall, across the Tamar from the PDSWJR, was an interesting mining district between the river near Gunnislake and Callington to the west. Its transport needs produced the 3ft 6ins gauge East Cornwall Mineral Railway from Kelly Bray near Callington to the Tamar at Calstock, opened in 1872. Mining however was in decline, here as elsewhere in Cornwall, and in 1894 the mineral railway sold out to the PDSWJR. The latter had a hard time raising the money to bridge the Tamar at Calstock and to join the regauged mineral line with its Lydford - Plymouth section. However, they managed it by 1908 and their Callington branch thereafter continued to carry traffic under successive owners until 1966. Its western end was then closed, leaving only the connection from Bere Alston on the Devon side of the river, to Gunnislake. This is still open. Having been built as a narrow gauge mineral railway the Callington line was a sharply curved affair with many speed restrictions. Latterly it was worked by 02 class LSW 0-4-4 tanks and LMS-type 2-6-2 tanks built by BR. Today a diesel railcar suffices for the Plymouth - Gunnislake services. The three miles from Calstock to Gunnislake is all that is left of the Southern in Cornwall.

Although in Cornwall, Bude was at the end of its own branch but is not included in this volume. It is fully described in *Branch Line to Bude* (Middleton Press).

90. Between 1886 and 1943 the two railways serving Launceston were not connected with rails, though from 1917 there was only one signal box. In 1943 wartime needs necessitated a physical connection between the SR and the GWR, and in 1952 BR concentrated all traffic at the SR station in the foreground. The GWR train behind will have worked their branch service from Plymouth. (Lens of Sutton)

91. In this post-nationalisation view we are looking in the opposite direction, with N class 2-6-0 no. 31830 at the west end of the station with a goods train. Evidence of the new status of the former SR station is in the shape of a GWR four-wheeled platform trolley on the left, beside a pair of the old LSWR high-wheeled type standing on their noses in the background. (Lens of Sutton)

92. Although the N class Maunsell Moguls had been the first modern engines on the North Cornwall line for many years, that was before the war. After it Bulleid Light Pacifics appeared. Working two coach trains was not evidence of weakness; merely a way of getting no. 34011 *Tavistock* to Padstow for a heavier return task. (T.Gough)

LISKEARD, CAUSELAND and LOOE

Miles		Week Days																	Sundays					
		am S	am	am S	am E	am S	am S	am S	am E	am	pm	pm	pm	pm E	pm	pm S	pm E	pm S	pm S	am	am	pm	pm	pm	pm
—	Liskeard .. .. dep	550	7 15	8 45	8 55	9 52	10 5	1125	1155	1 23	2 52	4 35	4 40	5 50	555	7 45	9 13	9 0	1035	12 15	2 10	4 35	7 40
2	Coombe Junction Halt ..	..	7 23	9 55	9 3	10 5	1015	1133	12 5	1 33	3 4	4 45	4 50	5 59	6 47	5 49	22	9 8	1043	12 23	2 18	4 43	7 48
3¼	St. Keyne Halt	..	7 28	9 0	9 8	1010	1021	1138	1210	1 36	3 8	4 50	4 55	6 4	6 9	7 58	9 26	9 13	1048	12 28	2 23	4 48	7 53
5	Causeland Halt	..	7 32	9 5	9 12	1014	1026	1142	1214	1 40	3 12	4 54	4 59	6 8	6 13	8 2	9 30	9 17	1052	12 32	2 27	4 52	7 57
6¼	Sandplace Halt	..	7 37	9 9	9 17	1019	1030	1146	1220	1 45	3 16	4 58	5 3	6 12	6 17	8 7	9 35	9 22	1057	12 37	2 31	4 57	8 2
8¼	Looe .... arr	620	7 44	9 17	9 24	1026	1037	1155	1228	1 53	3 23	5 5	5 10	6 20	625	8 14	9 42	9 30	11 5	12 45	2 40	5 5	8 10

Miles		Week Days																	Sundays					
		am S	am	am S	am E	am S	am S	am E	pm S	pm	pm	pm	pm N	pm E	pm S	pm S	am	am	pm	pm	pm	pm
—	Looe .. .. — .. dep	635	7 50	8 10	8 40	9 30	9 45	1045	1215	1240	2 0	345	5 10	6 30	6 45	8 30	9 50	9 45	11 20	1 25	2 50	6 30	8 20
2¼	Sandplace Halt	..	7 56	8 16	..	9 35	9 50	1050	1221	1246	2 6	351	5 16	6 35	6 50	8 36	9 55	9 51	11 26	1 30	2 56	6 36	8 26
3¾	Causeland Halt	..	3 0	8 20	..	9 39	9 54	1054	1225	1250	2 10	355	5 20	6 39	6 54	8 40	9 59	9 55	11 30	1 34	3 0	6 40	8 30
5	St. Keyne Halt ... ... —..	..	3 4	8 24	..	9 43	9 58	1058	1229	1254	2 14	4 0	5 24	6 43	6 58	8 44	10 3	9 59	11 34	1 38	3 4	6 44	8 34
6¾	Coombe Junction Halt ...	..	8 14	8 32	..	9 53	10 6	11 6	1236	1 2	2 21	410	5 33	6 51	7 6	3 51	1010	10 7	11 42	1 47	3 12	6 52	8 42
8¼	Liskeard .... arr	7 58	8 24	8 42	9 10	10 2	1017	1117	1246	1 11	2 33	420	5 44	7 1	7 16	9 1	1021	1016	11 52	1 58	3 22	7 1	8 51

E Except Saturdays   N 5 minutes later on Saturdays   S Saturdays only

93. The West Country Pacifics shared with the much older T9 class 4-4-0s the working of the day to day passenger service over the North Cornwall line. This is the 9.56am Okehampton to Padstow at Camelford (for Boscastle and Tintagel) on 15th July 1960. It averaged 27 mph on its 62 mile run. (R.C.Riley)

94. The lucky photographer hopped onto the footplate and rode with the crew to Delabole, where he ran to the ladder of the starting signal and captured no. 30719 and train again. As the 9.56am was the only train of the morning, apart from a very early departure from Okehampton, it was popular with local travellers and Delabole is doing a respectable trade. (R.C.Riley)

95. No. 31830 was sent to the West Country when new in 1926 and didn't leave until 1962, so its appearance twice in this section is not suprising. These small wheeled Moguls could manage a fair turn of speed for short periods, yet were powerful enough for the heavy gradients of the North Cornwall line. Shortly before the engine's transfer to Brighton, we see it entering Port Isaac Road from the east. (T.Gough)

96. Before the grouping brought Maunsell Moguls to North Cornwall, most trains were operated by Drummond's small wheeled 4-4-0s like no. 341 of class K10. Even in those far-off days before the first World War, photographers were rare enough at North Cornwall stations like St. Kew Highway - for everybody to look at the camera. Notice how short this train from Okehampton is. (Lens of Sutton)

97. As the 4.32pm local train from Bodmin (North), worked by O2 class no. 30236, arrives at Wadebridge, one of the renowned Beattie Well Tanks waits patiently as station pilot.

98. At the other end of Wadebridge station and going back to about 1930, a well kept T9 is about to leave on the last part of its journey to Padstow. Of the features visible we may notice the concrete signal post on the left contrasting with the traditional LSWR metal lattice one in the right foreground, and the distinctive LSWR water column. The station lighting is still gas. (Lens of Sutton)

99. Another, and less well kept, T9 waits to leave Wadebridge for Padstow on 4th September 1957. The corridor carriages are SR stock of 1935 vintage, painted in the BR red and cream colours. Non-corridor stock seemed to be a rarity on the North Cornwall line, perhaps because an end-to-end journey could take nearly three hours.

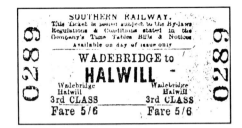

100. For such a small place, there always seemed to be plenty going on at Wadebridge; perhaps the proximity of the engine shed had something to do with it. Photographers on a pilgrimage were generally delighted to find one of the Well Tanks acting as station pilot. Here, some vans which have arrived from the North Cornwall line behind an N class Mogul, visible in the distance, are being detached for unloading.

101. Well Tank no. 30587 disgraced itself in 1957, or maybe it was run into by another engine. The result is that its wheels and cylinder cladding have been taken away and it stands outside the engine shed propped up on timbers. Was this the locomotive equivalent of being put in the stocks? Perhaps because only it and no. 30585 normally worked to Wenford Bridge, it was repaired and forgiven.

102. Padstow opened in 1899, and the neat stone signal box was contemporary with the station. By 1957 it still retained its LSWR nameboard, but the starting signal had acquired an SR upper quadrant arm on the original post. The last train of the day, the 6.00pm local to Okehampton, stands ready to leave. It could be romanticised as "The Up Mail", for it is complete with a van for mails brought to each station along the line by the local postman at the end of his day's work.

103. The Bodmin & Wadebridge Railway once had ambitions to serve the tin mining district near Lanivet, and a branch southwards to Ruthern Bridge was the result. It left the "main line" round the curve behind the train (5.11pm Wadebridge to Bodmin) and after rounding the sharp curve hidden by the bushes behind the hut, reappeared where the path is on the left. The LSWR eased the curve after the takeover and opened Grogley Halt (behind the camera) in 1906. The Ruthern Bridge line was lifted in 1934 and Grogley Halt closed in 1967.

104. Nanstallon was another of the 1906 halts on the Bodmin & Wadebridge. It had a level crossing, a signal box, and a siding, as well as the platform beyond the signal on a concrete gantry. This short goods working is being taken to Wadebridge by no. 30587.

105. There were two junctions at Boscarne, and this is the no. 1, nearer Wadebridge. The line to the GWR station at Bodmin is nearest the camera and no. 30236, heading a train for Bodmin (North) SR, has just left the single line from Wadebridge. No. 30585 has come from Wenford Bridge and is standing on the SR/GWR interchange siding, waiting to go forward to Wadebridge.

106. The white hut is Boscarne Juction No. 2 (Dunmere Junction) where the Wenford Bridge branch left the line to Bodmin (North). Here no. 30585 is just coming off the branch with a train consisting of empty coal trucks, sheeted open wagons with china clay, and one or two vans, fairly typical of the traffic in September 1957.

107. This is the final picture in a trio which includes nos. 97 and 103, for the train shown in them is seen here leaving Bodmin (North) on its second run, at 5.48pm. In fact duty no. 636 handled the Bodmin/Wadebridge "evening rush hour" single handed, making 2½ return trips with some of the turn round times being under 10 mins. Bodmin (North) had ample siding accomodation, but only one platform. It closed in 1967.

108. China clay came from the "dries" (driers) at Wenford Bridge bagged in covered vans, and sheeted in open wagons (on the right). This was the original terminus of the Bodmin & Wadebridge "main line" with sea sand from the Camel estuary being the principal traffic. A large granite quarry was opened later, reached by a 1 in 8 incline, the bottom of which is hidden by the buildings. SR local instructions were carefully drafted to ensure that no runaways from the incline got onto SR tracks.

109. On 3rd September 1957, as on all other trips, water was taken at Pencarrow Wood from this iron tank, supported on a trestle of old rails and fed by a stream. The engine's tank filler nestles among the coal in the bunker, which could cause problems if its lid was not replaced carefully. Two other features of no. 30585 are worthy of notice: the stowage of the fire irons and the (split) wooden buffer beam. It would appear that the branch platelayers had no motor trolley. Bicycles were the order of the day.

110. "Dunmere Crossing. Before a mineral train passes over the road from Bodmin to Wadebridge at Dunmere Crossing, situated at the foot of Dunmere Hill, it must be brought to a stand and the engine whistle sounded freely. The Guard must also stand at the crossing, in good view of the roadway, and exhibit a red flag until the train has passed over the crossing, as a warning to motorists descending the hill." This SR instruction clearly dates from a time when rail vehicles had far better brakes than those on the road. On this occasion there was no red flag, but a sufficiency of white shirts and braces.

111. In the last years of steam on the Callington branch, power was provided by LMS-type 2-6-2 tanks, quite unlike the GWR variety. This is the scene at Callington upon the arrival of the 5.23pm from Bere Alston on 18th August 1959. The passenger line ended at the buffer stops with no run-round facility, so either the empty train had to be backed out or another engine attached at the far end.

112. There was no turntable at Callington either, so tank engines were normally used on the branch. Callington station was actually at a place called Kelly Bray, an uphill mile or more from the town. No. 41315 is backing the 6.20pm to Bere Alston into the platform for loading, beside a minute signal box and a wooden post signal which was a relic of the Plymouth, Devonport & South Western Junction Railway.

113. The line at Luckett (previously Monks Corner and later Stoke Climsland) skirted the north side of Kit Hill, with tin and copper mines above and below the railway. They and others nearby led to the building of the narrow gauge East Cornwall Minerals Railway in 1872 which was re-born, standard gauge, in 1908. By 1959 mineral traffic and the mines were long in the past.

114. The wayside stations on the branch preserved their "light railway" air until the end. Latchley started life as a Cox's Park depot and once, like Luckett, had a siding and goods shed on the right. By 1959 it didn't even merit gates on the level crossing, cattle grids keeping livestock, but not photographers, off the track.

115. There is a passenger, and platform lighting, at Chilsworthy as the 2-6-2 tank hauling LSWR and SECR coaches calls with the teatime train from Bere Alston. There were mines here too, down in the valley of Tamar on the left, with the fabulous Devon Great Consols beneath the trees in the distance.

116. The approach to Gunnislake's island platform was by a subway beneath the tracks at the Calstock end of the station. The SR presence was more obvious here than elsewhere on the line, with the standard pattern of station equipment like lampposts and totem signs. Gunnislake too was once surrounded indeed undermined - with mineral workings.

117. Still looking towards Calstock but from the other end of the platform, we can see the original PDSWJR buildings of 1908 still very much in use in 1959. Goods sidings actively employed flank the passenger lines, on one side accommodating a standard SR brake van in the light grey livery used for stock not fitted with the vacuum brake.

118. Brake power, rather than haulage, was the need of this goods train approaching the steep gradient from Gunnislake down to Calstock. The ECMR had an incline but the standard gauge line avoided it by a 2¾ mile roundabout route. The engines in the downpour are O2 class no. 30193 and 2-6-2 tank no. 41315.

119. Far better weather prevailed at Calstock when the 6.20pm from Callington called, with one SR corridor composite brake accompanying two pre-Grouping coaches and providing the guard's accommodation. The SR also appears in the shape of totem signs and an early concrete running-in board.

120. Watched by a local resident, the Callington branch train leaves Cornwall by the Calstock viaduct over the Tamar, and heads for Bere Alston in glorious Devon.

MP **Middleton Press**

Easebourne Lane, Midhurst, West Sussex, GU29 9AZ
Tel: (0730) 813169 Fax: (0730) 812601

Companion albums in this style for other West of England lines

Branch Lines ...
Branch Line to Bude
Branch Lines to Exmouth
Branch Line to Lyme Regis
Branch Line to Lynton
Branch Line to Minehead
Branch Lines to Seaton and Sidmouth
Branch Line to Swanage to 1992
Branch Lines around Weymouth
(Abbotsbury, Easton and The Quay Tramway)

Southern Main Lines ...
Exeter to Barnstaple
Salisbury to Yeovil
Yeovil to Exeter

Country Railway Routes ...
Bath to Evercreech Junction
Bournemouth to Evercreech Junction
Burnham to Evercreech Junction

Tramway Classics ...
Exeter and Taunton Tramways

Write or telephone for the full list of Southern Classics